## The Royal Academy (TRAC)

One of the oldest and leading academic institutions in the Emirate of Ajman is located close to Sharjah and Umm Al Quwain. It was founded and is managed by The Lazar Group (TLG), a group that has been rendering quality education in the Northern Emirates of The United Arab Emirates since 1985. The Royal Academy is affiliated to the Central Board of Secondary Education, New Delhi, India and is recognized by the Ministry of Education, UAE. The school follows the prestigious Indian CBSE Curriculum from KG to Grade 12. One of the strongest features of the institution is that it has gained acceptance in society for its international standards of education, at an extremely economical price. Qualified, well experienced, and dedicated staff are the strength of the campus, in imparting wholesome education to the students under their care.

English Language
Galactic Adventures and Whimsical Whispers
(Stories & Poems)
by
Royal Authors

Published in November 2023
by Decan Imprint Publishing Co.
Reg. Off: Sharjah Publishing City
Free Zone Sharjah, UAE.
Phone: 00971-551830334
Email : decanimprint@gmail.com

**Cover Painting** : Syeda Rofia (Grade 10 A)

**Cover Design** : Prasanth Mangad

Printed at
Manipal Technologies Ltd.



09/23-24/SI.No.09/150/NS 18.6
ISBN 978-93-5973-919-9

# GALACTIC ADVENTURES AND WHIMSICAL WHISPERS

## A Kaleidoscope of Tales and verses

## Royal Authors

DECANIMPRINT

# CHAIRMAN'S MESSAGE

## Mr. Lanson Lazar

Language and Literature have always been the foundation and pillars of cultural understanding, artistic expression, and intellectual growth. This compilation embodies the vibrant tapestry of our students' literary work.

I extend my sincere appreciation and gratitude to the editors and reviewers who worked diligently in bringing this work to fruition. Their meticulous attention to detail and commitment to academic excellence have assured the quality and significance of this publication. May this compiled version of articles ignite your passion for language and literature, provoke new heights and inspire lifelong love for the written word.

Writers, editors, proofreaders, designers, and many others have dedicated their time and expertise to ensure quality and integrity of the content.

I would like to express my deepest gratitude to our student writers whose passion and dedication have made this publication a reality. Your contributions, dear students, have enriched the literary landscape. Creativity has no limits, hence the transformation of this literary landscape will continue.

Together let us continue to embrace our students' passion for writing to build a brighter future for them, as well as for society.

# CEO's MESSAGE
## Ms. Sandra Blaskovic

Language, the cornerstone of human communication, be it spoken or written, has the power to shape societies, bridge cultural gaps and unlock profound potential.

It is with great pleasure that we present this significant literary work of our students. From the preliminary conception of the idea to the final publication, the journey of this book has been a collaborative effort involving several passionate individuals.

I would like to express my deepest gratitude to our student writers, whose love for writing has made this anthology a reality. Their contributions have enriched the literary panorama and expanded imaginary horizons, at the same time our writers will enjoy increased visibility and valuable experience. This compilation not only celebrates creativity and expression but is also aimed at making it a reader's delight.

Thank you for joining us on this intellectual literary journey, a testimony to the enduring value of literature. Together let us celebrate the beauty, complexity and love of language and embrace its transformative power in shaping the world.

# PRINCIPAL'S MESSAGE
## Mr.E.V. Shakkeer Hussain

Language is not something that to mug up and get marks.

Language is a great tool to express. We sculpt our students for the same reason. We were not expecting this kind of response when we formed The Royal Writer's Forum, which created more than 19 blooming writers who published their books. And yet another milestone by producing this anthology too

I am delighted to introduce our school anthology, a labour of love and creativity that showcases the remarkable talents of our students.

To our young authors and artists, I extend my heartfelt congratulations. Your contributions to this anthology are not only a source of pride for you but also a source of inspiration for your peers. Your work embodies the very essence of our school's mission: to foster creativity, critical thinking, and a love of learning.

To the parents and guardians, I want to express my gratitude for your unwavering support of your children's creative endeavors.

Lastly, I want to acknowledge the dedication and hard work of our teachers who have nurtured and guided our students.

Thank you for being a part of this incredible journey, and I hope you find inspiration, joy, and a deeper appreciation for the creative spirit that thrives within our school.

# CONTENTS


- BELLA'S DREAM — 13
  *Yusra (Gr. 6B)*
- BOOK OF NIGHT — 14
  *Marium Mehnaz (Gr.11B)*
- FACES — 15
  *Shania Anne (Gr.10B)*
- FAIRIES — 16
  *Ayaan Ahmed (Gr.4D)*
- MEMORIES OF LIFE — 17
  *Jude Henriques (Gr.11B)*
- PERSEVERANCE AMIDST THE STRUGGLE: A STUDENT'S JOURNEY — 18
  *Sayada Jafran (Gr. 11A)*
- PERTINACITY — 19
  *Mystica (Gr.10B)*
- THE GREAT ESCAPE — 20
  *Joshna (Gr. 7B)*
- THE SUPERHERO! — 22
  *Aruvela Akshaya (Gr. 5B)*
- THE YING YANG OF LIFE — 23
  *Asni Nasar (Gr. 12B)*
- TWO FACES OF LIFE — 25
  *Shahin Banu (Gr. 11B)*
- STUBBORN HUMAN HEARTS — 26
  *Arwa Khalil (Gr. 11A)*

- FROM TRASH TO TREASURE:     27
  UPCYCLING IN FASHION AND DESIGN
  *Amani Balisi (Gr.11)*
- THE TURTLE WHO LOST ITS HOME     30
  *Maryam Abdul Samid (Gr. 6C)*
- HOLIDAYS     31
  *Abhijeet Saha (Gr.8)*
- CALLOUS     32
  *Salwa Hasim (Gr.11B)*
- MARS – OUR NEXT HOME!     33
  *Samira Mohammed (Gr. 10A)*
- THE JOURNEY TO BECOME A BUTTERFLY     35
  *Samra Mariyam Shanavas (Gr. 10B)*
- TO MY BELOVED FRIEND     36
  *Ayesha Mohammad Shuaib Khan (Gr.10B)*
- GRIEVING     37
  *Archana Mohan (Gr. 10B)*
- FOREST GIRL     38
  *NairaSheikh(Gr. 6C)*

- EDITORIAL     39
  *Roopa Bhalla*

# BELLA'S DREAM
## Yusra (Gr. 6B)

Once upon a time, there was a girl named Bella who loved flowers. When she was 10 years old, her school teacher took a chapter in English, about 'Flower Gardens'. It was a very interesting lesson. That day in class, she got the idea to make a flower garden in her home. She was quite excited.

In the afternoon after reaching home, she took a bath, had her lunch, and rested for a while. In the evening, she stepped outside and found a place to plant the flowers. She planted them with such joy. The next day morning, before going to school she watered the plants.

After a few days, when she looked at the plants, they had grown. After two weeks, on one plant, she noticed a bud and she was very happy.When she told her mom, her mom told her that the bud would turn into a flower some days later. Bella was very happy on hearing this.

Exam time came and she got busy studying

So she forgot about watering her plants! After the exam when she went to her flower garden all the plants had dried up! On seeing this, she was very upset and cried all night thinking about her dream that was not going to work.

In the morning her mother said, "Don't be sad my dear. You can always make your dream come true. I will help you. Don't stop doing anything because of failing. Never give up! There is always another chance. So, come on and start your flower garden all over again." That was just the motivation she required, and Bella started preparing for her flower garden, all over again.

# BOOK OF NIGHT

## Marium Mehnaz (Gr.11B)

In the pages of books
Let me write and you hear.
In my words I say,
Maybe I will make your day.
Talking and smiling with you
 will be turned into a story,
which you will never know,
when it was all because of me.
I take glances at you,
words written in the books.
You might never know,
when it was all because of the looks.
I don't know how and what to write,
but I will stay with you all through the night.

# FACES

## Shania Anne (Gr.10B)

Everybody has two faces.
Including me and you.
One that's loved by all and
One that hurts you, not thinking,
How you feel at all.
It's strange, but true and
Will certainly fool you.
As the same person who loved you,
Can be the reason you hate yourself.
I know it's hard to see, but
believe me, people have two faces,
I have seen it myself, indeed.

# FAIRIES

## Ayaan Ahmed (Gr.4D)

Fairies are lonely but beautiful.
They have bright and glittery eyes.
Eyes that shine and skin of a fair complexion.
They have beautiful big wings.
They can fly high and touch the skies.

# MEMORIES OF LIFE
## Jude Henriques (Gr.11B)

I was obsessed with picture-perfect.
I searched the world inside and out,
For a single moment, I could say,
My life was viewed through lenses.
My camera a medal won with pride,
Though it held the moments,
That I'd always keep inside.
But looking back at the photos,
I can't remember how I felt,
The noises that the world had made,
Or the way the warm air smelt,
I don't remember how the day was,
Whether it was good or bad.
I have just a snapshot of the moment,
That nobody even had.
So, I gave away my camera,
And now I use my eyes instead,
To take photos for the scrapbook,
That I've made inside my head,
I always thought my photos,
Were ways to make my moments last,
But you remember life way better,
When you don't view it all through glass.

# PERSEVERANCE AMIDST THE STRUGGLE: A STUDENT'S JOURNEY

**Sayada Jafran (Gr. 11A)**

In shadows deep, she finds her way,
A girl of strength, with colors that sway.
Through trials harsh, she stands so tall,
In the face of bullies, she won't fall.
With words unkind, they try to break,
But she's a flame that cannot shake.
Her spirit shines, a radiant light,
Defying darkness, with all her might.
In her heart, courage so rare,
She knows her worth, beyond compare.
No bully's words can dim her grace,
For she's a masterpiece, in every space.
So, rise, brave girl, let your voice be heard,
You're stronger than hate, defying the absurd.
With love and strength, your path is clear,
A shining example, for all to cheer.

# PERTINACITY

## Mystica (Gr.10B)

She, a living inspiration to every female.
Her success made one and all pale.
She never broke down from life's intense choices.
Within her, the pertinacity rises!
She won the world record for achieving her dream,
And all with grace she gleams!
She climbed the Mt. Everest twice,
With her courage and confidence on the rise!

# THE GREAT ESCAPE
## Joshna (Gr. 7B)

There lived a girl named Nisha, whose father and mother worked quite far from home. They reach home from work only after 8 pm. Nisha's school bus comes early, at 6 am. Being so early, usually there was no one in that area.

One day, when she was waiting for her bus, a van came and stopped near her. The next thing she realized was, a person suddenly shoving a handkerchief on her nose and mouth. When she woke up, she was in a room with a door, a trapdoor, a table, and one small window. She saw two other children, Safa, and John, also trapped in the same room. They told her that they too had been kidnapped and that they were in an abandoned warehouse.

Many other children had also been kidnapped and trapped in various warehouses, in the same manner. Almost an hour later, Nisha became restless. She looked around. There must be a way out, she thought.  She asked Safa and John if they knew of any way out. They said that quite often one of the kidnappers would come into check on them.  The kidnapper had the keys to the door and the trapdoor, in his pocket. They thought of a plan; two of them would distract the kidnapper, and one of them would quietly take the keys to the trapdoor and they could escape.  They were not quite sure where the trapdoor would lead them to, but it was worth a try.

After about an hour, a masked kidnapper came in. Nisha and Safa pretended to plead with the kidnapper to let them go. Meanwhile, John quietly went up to the kidnapper and stealthily took the key from his pocket. The kidnapper ignored the pleas of the other two, pushed them aside, checked the room, and left. A few moments later, the three children opened the trapdoor and escaped through it. Luckily, the warehouse was not far from Nisha's house.

It was 9 pm by the time they got home. Nisha's parents were very worried and asked why she was so late and who the two children were. Nisha narrated the whole incident. They called Safa's and John's parents who were equally worried. They came immediately and took them home. Later, they called the police and reported the incident. The police soon started searching for the kidnappers.

A few days later, they were found and arrested. News reached her neighborhood, and everyone praised her Nisha for her cleverness and bravery. The next day evening, while she was playing with her friends, and telling them all about how she escaped from the room, she saw a girl near the shop. A van stopped near her for a while and then left. The girl was not there anymore. The next day, she saw posters on the walls and streetlight poles saying that the girl was missing. She took a closer look. It was the same girl she saw yesterday near the shop. She started to wonder, was she kidnapped too? She thought to herself,maybe there was another group of even more experienced kidnappers, somewhere out there!

# THE SUPERHERO!
## Aruvela Akshaya (Gr. 5B)

In the sky nobody can fly.
The person who can fly high,
Up Up! In the silent sky
Up Up! In the silent sky
And rend the windlike a bird
Who has no fear in the sky.
Sometime have flying trouble
But who beat and rush in his own style
That man only walks on the sky
Ya Ya! He is a pilot.

# THE YING YANG OF LIFE
## Asni Nasar (Gr. 12B)

Tell me when will our minds feel free again?
When can I sleep without looking at the time again?
When can I cry and feel comforted again?
When can I try and have my effort seen again?
When can I smile again?
I want you to smile for me again,
Do it gently they said
I was once friendly
but now the societal standard has gotten to me,
and now I feel everything is expected of me.
I've forgotten the time when I didn't have any
pressure
when the little things were the real pressure!
the seashells on the beach shore,
making art and craft with the t-shirt that tore,
time we used to spend with family more
but no expectations of other is important
'the life core'
money, fame and many more.
But are these things worth trading for peace of
mind?
"either are"
"Neither nor"
All these rigid rules have made me go through pain
and now numb.

It's sad how those who don't fall in the categories
are labeled 'dumb.'

Isn't it sad what we have made from the world that
the lord has given us?

We made systems that don't even include us

Yet as the years pass, I want to reach a good position
in life.

# TWO FACES OF LIFE
**Shahin Banu (Gr. 11B)**

Whenever you are sad, angry or
stressed look at those two faces, who
worry for you but no one else.
They always want you to be happy with a charming
smile because you are theirs!
The one man who works at night and sacrifices
his joy and buys what all you need.
He is dad.
Another who cares for you like no one else does.
Her eyes are filled with tears when you're down.
It's your Mom.
When you talk to them with a happy smile
they feel stress-free and put a beautiful smile
on their faces.
Who is their best friend?
 It's you.

## STUBBORN HUMAN HEARTS
**Arwa Khalil (Gr. 11A)**

I will hurt you.
Of course, you will hurt me.
And that's the meaning of reality.
To receive happiness the
Pain will present itself.
And every so often comes the ease.

# FROM TRASH TO TREASURE: UPCYCLING IN FASHION AND DESIGN
### Amani Balisi (Gr.11)

Did you know that the fashion industry ranks as the second-largest polluter, globally? This surprising fact has sparked increasing interest in recycling within the fashion industry. The recycle in fashion where plastics, rubber, paper, glass, old clothes, and fabrics are transformed into trendy, stylish and eco-friendly designs that does not only look great for fashion but also tells us about a powerful message for the future of our planet. In this article we will dive more into the world of upcycling in the fashion industry by exploring its upcycling techniques, challenges, advantages, and the creative thinkers behind this eco-friendly movement.

## Upcycling Techniques

There are various methods to transform existing materials into new, stylish, and eco-friendly products. For example, patchwork,where we combine various fabric scraps or pieces to create a unique design. We can also cut and reconstruct by turning jeans into shorts. We can also repair the damaged clothes by adding patches. Another technique is to add buttons or old jewelry.

## Challenges faced by upcycled fashion

Finding a steady supply of premium upcycled material can be challenging and maintaining a good quality in upcycled products can be difficult as we are using old existing materials. Also, it's also hard to convince consumers to buy these products as they are more likely to buy a product which is very high quality and competing with fashion brands these days who offer cheaper and trendy items is very hard. As we know that upcycling within the fashion industry is supposed to eliminate waste, it actually may not eliminate waste entirely as there are some materials which may be unusable and non-recyclable.

## Advantages

There are various advantages for upcycling in fashion and designs. First,it's eco-friendly which is good for our planet. It reduces chemical use, water usage and waste. This also helps and supports local artisans, creates jobs, and gives many opportunities to people, it's educational and it changes the fashion industry to something new.

## Creative Thinkers

Katherine Hamnett one of the many British designers who is known for her upcycled materials in her designs back in the 1980s. She incorporated military surplus and vintage fabrics creating new pieces.

There are various local artisans and DIY enthusiasts who showcase their creativity through platforms like Shopify and Etsy, these are some of the platforms where handmade and upcycled fashion items succeed. Collaboration is a big thing in the fashion industry it's a way for more than one person to increase creativity and many levels and collaboration in the fashion industry can also work with collaborating eco-friendly brands to promote and give awareness for instance H&M who has partnered with various eco-friendly brands promoting upcycling fashion.

Ultimately, upcycling is more than just fashion and trends, it's a message and a movement for a more sustainable and creative future. The recycling of materials which instead of being thrown and being a waste can be used to transform into creative and unique fashion and designs which are a good way to give awareness for our environment and benefit both the people and the planet. So next time you're contemplating a fashion purchase, always remember that treasure can often be found where you least expect it to be.

# THE TURTLE WHO LOST ITS HOME
## Maryam Abdul Samid (Gr. 6C)

Once upon a time there was a turtle named Ricky. He was very naughty and playful. Ricky always played with his best friend Pinky who was very good and always listening to others.

One day Ricky decided to go on a journey off to the mountains, without the permission of his mother Wham.

Pinky heard about this, and Pinky said, "We must ask our parents' permission as the mountains are very dangerous.We don't want to get lost, do we?" As Ricky heard this, it said, "Come on, we are not small children anymore. Besides we won't get lost as we know the path to our home." Pinky agreed to go to the mountains, but she had a feeling that they were going to be lost! On the day they were going, she took some small pebbles and put them in her bag.

Ricky and Pinky set off on their journey. Pinky started to drop the pebbles one by one. Soon they came across a thick forest which was quite scary. Ricky looked and said,"I think we should go home. It looks very scary here!" Pinky agreed and nodded. As they turned back Ricky knew he had forgotten the path home. Pinky was smart! She looked for the pebbles she had dropped on the way. Pinky led the way and Ricky followed her. They reached home safely.

On reaching home, their parents asked them where they went. Looking quite sheepish, Ricky said that they had gone up to the mountains and had got lost, but with Pinky's thoughtfulness, they were able to find their way home and thanked God that Pinky had carried along the small pebbles. Otherwise, they would have been lost! They were also apologetic for not getting permission from their parents. Mother said, "It's okay to make mistakes. We learn from our mistakes. So, remember, next time let us know before you do something, so that we can advise you."

# HOLIDAYS

## Abhijeet Saha (Gr.8)

The long-awaited holidays had come back.
Life's train is again onits joyful track!
A time full of fun and games,
Once again, we will light our creativity flame!

It's a time of 'free from tension'.
It's a time of beginning all our creation.
After a long period of wear and tear,
We got freetime, we searched everywhere.

The weather is so calm.
Everything aroundis full of charm!
Now even we may play in the rain,
Cause there is no tension, of falling ill in our brain!

# CALLOUS
## Salwa Hasim (Gr.11B)

The conviction that feels unreal has an impact on her,
Despite her stern veins that are impassive or sheer.
For bye if her pores bother you, her heart might too,
coz it's filled with undesired words and scratches,
And bruises and holes rolling deep inside.
Fetching the roots to make her unloving and discourteous,
so, she hopes only to sit-aside,
wishing at best of shutting one's eye,
To even wonder of her ilk,
for at time their long suffering might cure her.
"Yes, I'm back," she said," but not sure for how long."

# MARS – OUR NEXT HOME!
## Samira Mohammed (Gr. 10A)

Yes, the bright reddish planet from our solar system which is next to our Earth will one day be our home! We can tell this from the fascinating research done by our researchers. It is interesting to see how the people of Earth are fascinated by the thought of creating Mars as their second home. In the history of exploration of space, Humans were always back of finding a next home after the earth. In this research, Mars was given great importance and considered as our next home. Some say it is a thrilling leap into the future while some consider it a thought-provoking adventure. In fact, about 34% of the population are waiting for the time when they will take their first step on the land of Mars. Have you ever wondered whether life on Mars will be the same as on earth? How will we manage to get all the resources that we are free to use on Earth?

Well, Mars has a variety of resources available that just need the proper technologies to be made handy, which again is no big deal for today's time. Surprisingly, Mars also has many valuable resources like water and minerals which can benefit humanity. Evidence also shows that Mars once was full of water, warmer and an appropriate atmosphere which was suitable to inhabit in. Hence, this gives us a hope of creating Mars as our next home. Stating about the interior structure of Mars is quite questionable. During the past years, we expected that the magnetic field of Mars will be strong as that of the Earth. But to our surprise, the magnetic field of the planet is comparatively weaker.

The plan of visiting Mars was made years ago. Mars exploration began in the 1960s by the USSR. The first successful flyby to Mars was on 14-15 July 1965, by NASA's Mariner 4. The second successful flyby to Mars was again by NASA's Mariner 6, on 25 February 1969. Hence, we can get an understanding that humans were always excited to know about Mars. Recently, NASA is hoping to settle the first humans on Mars by the 2030s. Meanwhile, the founder and CEO of SpaceX says it would take 1000 rockets and approximately 20 years to set up a self-sustaining city on Mars. Moreover, he predicts that a crewed mission to Mars will be conducted in 2029. In the year 2016, Elon musk stated that a 'meaningful number of people' could reach the red planet.

What is the main idea behind all the research on Mars, you might wonder? Stephen Hawking once said, "I don't think the human race will survive the next thousand years, unless we spread into space." Overpopulation is an enormous issue in the world today. Another main reason for this is for the search of life, understanding the surface and preparing for the future for human exploration. Scientists are in search of the answer to the question, whether life existed elsewhere in the Universe beyond Earth. To get an accurate answer to this question, Mars is an excellent place to investigate as it has shown many similarities to that of Earth.

There was always a debate whether or not we should colonize Mars. According to some, choosing Mars for habitation is not so a good idea due to all the disadvantages that come along. Moving to Mars will require a great amount of finance. Also, the rate of carbon dioxide on the planet is high which can be risky. Living on another planet, like Mars, could ensure the survival and success of the human race, as it is a viable solution to the overpopulation on Earth, as well as the loss of resources. Now, it is all in the hands of time that will decide our future.

# THE JOURNEY TO BECOMING A BUTTERFLY

**Samra Mariyam Shanavas (Gr. 10B)**

We know growth takes time,
Yet we forget.
Why do we forget when it comes to ourselves?
Why be impatient when you can see the
Answerfor yourself with time?
Why worry if you are a caterpillar.
If you would eventually become a butterfly?
The Journey may take long,
But never long enough
As the Journey itself is spellbinding.

# TO MY BELOVED FRIEND
## Ayesha Mohammad Shuaib Khan (Gr.10B)

You came into my life as an unwelcome face,
Not ever knowing our friendship I would one day embrace.
As I wander through my thoughts and memories of you,
It brings me many big smiles and laughter so true.

I love the special bond that we beautifully share,
I love the way you show you really care.
Our friendship means the absolute world to me,
I hope this is something I can make you see.

Thank you for opening your mind and soul,
I will do all can to help you heal your heart's little holes.
Remember, your secrets are forever safe with me,
I will keep them under the tightest lock and key.

Thank you for trusting me from the start,
You truly have a beautiful heart.
I am now so happy that I felt that embrace,
For now, I see the beauty of my best friend's face

## GRIEVING
### Archana Mohan (Gr. 10B)

I have sat on the seashore and washed away my tears.
I have lived so many days now that
they are turning into years.
Why does it never feel right or,
Is it just me, or do the others feel the same too?
I looked at my scar and smiled at least the scar
on my hand is
Fading, unlike the pain in my heart

# FOREST GIRL

## Naira Sheikh (Gr. 6C)

Once upon a time, there was a girl named Lisa, who lived in Brazil. It was flled with greenery, the town surrounded by the luscious fora and fauna . Lisa was a very quiet girl who would mostly spend her time reading books or playing with the animals like cats and rabbits. She often went to a forest nearby their village to the point that she got the nickname "Forest Girl"

One day when she was coming back from school, she heard a bunny crying out. She put her bag down and started looking around. She then heard the sound coming from the more darker side of the forest, nevertheless she went into it and saw a bunny with its ears stuck on a branch. She quickly saved it and comforted the bunny. When she was about to head back, she realized she couldn't, as she had never been here before. She got scared by how dark it had become and so she curled up and started to cry.

But then suddenly she felt a sort of light and looked up to see a pixie. She couldn't believe it. It was too small to understand what it was saying but by the gestures, it was giving, Lisa knew it was trying to help her so she followed the pixie and eventually she saw her bag at a tree. She finally reached home! She thanked the pixie and got in home. Even though she never told the town about the pixie, whenever someone asked her how she got back, she always said "a small friend helped me."

# EDITORIAL
## Ms. Roopa Bhalla

Welcome to a realm where the boundaries of reality blur, and the celestial vastness intertwines with the magic of imagination. In "Galactic Adventures and Whimsical Whispers: A Kaleidoscope of Tales and Verses," we embark on a literary journey through the cosmos of adventure and the enchanting tapestry of human emotions and experiences.

Within these pages, you will traverse the farthest reaches of outer space, where the stars become the canvas for intrepid tales of exploration and discovery. Brace yourself for adrenaline-pumping expeditions, intergalactic mysteries, and the marvels that await beyond our planet's atmosphere. These short stories will transport you to a universe of awe and wonder, where the infinite possibilities of the cosmos ignite the flames of adventurous spirit within us all.

Yet, nestled amidst the interstellar odysseys are delicate and heartfelt verses that celebrate the nuanced beauty of faces, the ethereal allure of fairies, and the innocence of childhood memories. These poems weave the fabric of emotions, illuminating the cherished moments that define our lives. They are a gentle reminder of the simple joys found in the fleeting laughter of a child, the enchanting whispers of fairies, and the tender embrace of friendship.

As you read through these pages, you will encounter the joyful fervor of holidays, reliving the magic and excitement that these special occasions bring. These tales will rekindle the childlike wonder within, inviting you to experience the holidays anew, complete with their traditions, flavors, and enchantment.

In the realm of fantasy, where the impossible becomes possible, we delve into stories that defy reality and invite you to explore the boundaries of the known. Dragons, unicorns, and mythical realms await your discovery, filling the air with a sense of wonder and leaving a trace of magic in your heart.

Lastly, we delve into the intricacies of human connections, celebrating the beautiful tapestry of friendships that color our lives. The tales of companionship, camaraderie, and shared adventures underscore the importance of genuine relationships and the transformative power of true friendship.

"Galactic Adventures and Whimsical Whispers: A Kaleidoscope of Tales and Verses" is an invitation to dream, to soar through the cosmos, and to wander into the realms of fantasy. It beckons you to embrace the child within and see the world through the lens of wonder and awe once more. For in the fusion of adventure and imagination, we find the magic that keeps our spirits alive, forever young and forever hungry for the next tale, the next adventure, and the next dream.